THE FOUR SEASONS
OF GRIEF

A Journey of Loss, Healing and Renewal

S. Andrea Greene

ISBN: 9798858742586

Library of Congress Control Number: 2023916555

This book is a work of nonfiction. Unless otherwise noted, the author makes no explicit guarantees as to the accuracy of the information contained in this book and in some cases, names of people and places have been altered to protect their privacy.

Book cover design by Yasir Nadeem

https://www.soulsurvivors.net/

Acknowledgements

Thank you to my family for your love and support. Your presence, patience, listening ears and open arms helped guide me through my darkest hours. To my daughter and son, you have always been my inspiration and my reason to keep going. Granddaughter, thank you for refilling my heart with an abundance of love, warmth and gratitude. I am forever grateful that life gave us the gift of you. Auntie, thank you for suggesting I write this book.

Preface

The Four Seasons of Grief is a heartfelt exploration of the human experience and the universal journey of grieving. Through the metaphor of seasons, we learn that grief is not a linear path but a transformative, often cyclical, process. By embracing the lessons of each season, we can find solace, strength, and a renewed sense of purpose in our lives. This book is intended to serve as a guiding light, offering comfort, inspiration, and practical strategies for navigating the complex landscape of grief. May it provide clarity and relief to those who have lost, understanding to those who support them, and a gentle reminder to all that even in our darkest moments, there is hope for healing and growth.

Introduction

If you are reading this, it is likely that you or someone close to you is grappling with the profound loss of a loved one, and you may be seeking answers or taking a step in your healing journey. First and foremost, I want to extend my heartfelt compassion and support to you and all who are connected to you during this challenging time. Within the pages of this book, I aim to convey my sincere message to the wounded and brokenhearted, with the hope that reading it will bring you solace, strength, courage, and ultimately, guide you on a path toward rediscovering peace and joy.

The passing of a loved one can leave us feeling as though a part of us has died along with them. In a way, this is an accurate reflection of our experience. The vacant chair at the table, the absence during special occasions, and the void in our daily interactions all serve as poignant reminders that the life we once knew has irrevocably changed. Consequently, we, too, undergo a transformation. Our perspectives shift, and the altered bonds of love can inflict profound pain. I want to delve into the intricacies of this process, keeping in mind that everyone grieves differently. I encourage you to consider the advice I once received from a friend, "Eat the meat and leave the gristle." In other words, take what resonates with you and feel free to modify or disregard what does not as you navigate your unique journey through grief.

Moreover, it is essential to recognize that despite the weight of grief, there is life on the other side of it. Even in the midst of sorrow, life continues, and we have the potential to make the most of it, to grow through it as we go through it. I will be exploring this aspect in greater detail later on, but before doing so, I want to emphasize the significance of acknowledging and embracing the complexity of grief itself.

Let's take a closer look at the notion of grief as a multifaceted experience. While it is indeed a profound emotional response triggered by the loss of a loved one or something we hold dear, grief is not merely a single feeling or a static state. Instead, it manifests as a journey – an intricate and evolving process that unfolds over time. This journey can be unpredictable, encompassing a range of emotions, thoughts, and reactions. At times, you might feel overwhelmed by sadness and heartache, while at other moments, you might experience feelings of acceptance or even find solace in cherished memories. There is no prescribed path through grief; it is a deeply personal expedition that varies for each individual.

Throughout this book, I will explore the various aspects of the grief journey, offering insights, coping mechanisms, personal anecdotes, and gentle guidance to help you navigate through the challenging moments. By recognizing and embracing both the universal and unique aspects of your grief, you can take the first steps toward healing and rediscovering the fullness of life, even amidst sorrow.

In the following chapters, we will explore the dynamics of grief, develop an understanding of the stages that often accompany it, and uncover ways to honor and cherish the memory of your loved one while forging a new path forward. Remember, *healing is not about erasing the pain but finding ways to carry it with grace and resilience.* As you continue reading and moving forward, may you discover the strength within you to embrace the complexities of grief and embark on a transformative journey healing and renewal.

The pain of grief can be an all-encompassing force, whether it stems from losing a spouse, a parent, a child, a sibling, or even a close friend. When faced with loss, we often find ourselves desperately seeking answers to questions that have none. Death's inevitability reminds us of the aspects of life that are beyond our control, and this realization can be frightening. We grieve not only for the loved one we have lost, but also for the shared moments, the memories, and the dreams of the future that will never come to fruition. The finality of death can weigh upon us like an unbearable burden, as if we were carrying the worst of house guests who have taken residence in our heart and mind; an unwelcome visitor that arrives without invitation and turns daytime into long, cold nights.

Having lost a loved one, we find ourselves grappling with a multitude of emotions – pain, anger, fear, sadness, confusion, and often, overwhelming loneliness. It is essential to recognize that these feelings are an inherent part of the grief process. As the saying goes, there is a time and season for everything, including death and grief. However, what I want you to know is that despite the intensity of these emotions, you have the capacity to endure and, perhaps surprisingly, even grow through this experience. Our worst encounters in life often serve as our greatest teachers. They compel us to draw upon inner strengths and perseverance that we may not have been aware of. Consequently, as we journey through grief, we can emerge on the other side as individuals who are stronger, better, wiser, and more resilient.

Still, it is important to acknowledge that before the rainbow comes the rain. There is no escaping the difficulties on this road of grief. It is a personal journey that no one else can take on our behalf, and there are certain parts of this road that we must travel alone. My goal is to provide you with a supportive framework to help you identify where you currently are in your grief process. Furthermore, I hope to equip you with tools and coping mechanisms that will help you navigate through the seasons of grief, offering you a lifeline of survival until thriving once again becomes an option.

Through this book, I will walk with you as a companion on your journey, offering guidance and understanding, but ultimately, your strength, determination and resilience will carry you through. Grief is an individual experience, and no two paths are the same. But by walking together through the pages that follow, my hope is that you will find solace, clarity, and the knowledge that you are not alone in your grief. Together, we will explore the transformative power of healing and honor the memory of those we have lost by living our lives with purpose and grace.

In the echoes of love, grief finds its place,
A tango of memories, a tender embrace.
Through tears that flow like rivers deep,
Love's bonds endure, their promises keep.

And with every ache, love's pulse remains,
A garment that withstands all heartache's stains.
In grief's embrace we can learn to mend,
Love's thread unbroken, even in the end.

Winter

One fateful day in June, 2019, I received a call from my husband's sister. She was frantically explaining that she had received a call from another sibling with whom my husband had shared he was planning to end his life. Coincidentally, just as she spoke, I noticed his truck pulling into the driveway, exactly as it did every other day. I calmly reassured her, saying, "He's home," believing our home was a safe haven where such thoughts and actions had no place. In my mind, I pictured him going about his usual routine, unloading tools, having a cigarette, or a drink in his truck before coming inside. We'd had a serious disagreement earlier in the day so I assumed he was sulking or taking a moment to gather himself before talking to me. The last time we spoke, he told me he would be by the house later. In hindsight, it was not something he would normally say. But, at that moment, his word choice went completely unnoticed. At one point, I heard what sounded like an attempt to ring the doorbell. It was a slight ding, not a full ring. At the time, I was furious about what happened earlier, and doing something I had never done - vent to one of his sisters. Even the strange, unlikeliness of the two of us talking to each other didn't dawn on me at the time. I was just relieved to be able to share with someone in his family since, over the years, I rarely communicated with his siblings and when I did, interactions ranged from cursory to contentious. This conversation was neither. She expressed concern for her brother and asked if she could come down as she had vacation she'd planned to use. I was receptive and agreed to the visit. As we reached the end of our talk, she asked me to tell her brother to call her. I agreed and we ended the call.

After our conversation ended, I walked to the front of the house and looked through the glass panel next to the front door, but did not see him. Concerned, I walked to the back of the house and looked through the windows there to see if he was on the patio or in the yard. He wasn't there either. I thought, "Maybe he went for a walk or is talking to a neighbor", as he often did. I walked to the front door and stepped outside. There was a stillness, a sense of both presence and absence. As I turned and looked to the right, there he was, my husband of 15 years hanging from one of the pillars beside the front door. I rushed to him, desperately attempting to lift him and untie the rope. My efforts were futile, so I raced inside, grabbing a knife from the kitchen while dialing 911. I returned in seconds, cut him down and tried to perform CPR. I screamed for help at a time of day when it was common to see people jogging, walking in pairs or with children and pets.This day, there was no one to hear my cries. When the paramedics arrived, they tragically confirmed his passing. In an instant, my husband was gone, and I had unknowingly become a member of a club no one ever wants to join. I was a widow who lost her spouse to suicide. This reality was something I couldn't change or escape. Please allow the hardest, most hurtful lesson I have ever learned be a word of caution to all that may save someone else's life: **If someone you love threatens self harm, take nothing for granted. Seek help immediately.**

In the days that followed, I lived in a daze, hoping someone would shake me awake from the nightmare. Fear of the night's silence consumed me, leading me to stay mostly awake, drifting in and out of involuntary dozes, jolting myself awake each time. The nights seemed endless, and the room we shared for years now felt cold and empty. There was no note, no answers, no closure – only guilt, regret, and relentless wishing that things were different along with thoughts of "shoulda, woulda, coulda." Amidst the grief, anger arose, and I felt abandoned by him, left to grapple with the haunting question of "Why?" each day. Guilt compounded grief. I wondered how could I not have been there? How could I not have known? Why didn't I get to him sooner?

I felt as if I was wearing a scarlet letter of guilt, shame and sorrow, and no amount of scrubbing could erase it. It was a winter that began in June – the coldest and longest season of my life. My husband, just 50 years old, had promised me another 40 years. In a day, a moment of anger and despair, those dreams and plans were shattered and the promise, broken. It was unfathomable.

Despite the overwhelming pain, I clung to a determination that this tragedy would not claim both our lives. I knew I had to grieve, I was willing to go through the grief, but I made a conscious decision very early on not to allow the grief to overtake me to the point of physical or mental illness. Connectedness, love and a lingering sense of personal responsibility added to layers fell like snow. Thankfully, with the help of a loving family and great therapist, instead of succumbing, I adopted a mandate to grow from this experience, even when and especially because it sometimes felt like I was in an uphill battle for my mental, emotional, and physical survival. I held on to a story my father told me about two friends who went swimming. One friend began to drown and the other swam over to save him. As the one drowning began flailing his arms, striking his friend as he attempted to rescue him, pulling him under as he attempted to bring him to shore, the one friend had to decide if two people would drown that day. The truth of his message fell with the weight of a ton of bricks. Though you may try, it may not be possible to save everyone, particularly someone who is fighting the one trying to help. I am honest but careful with my husband's memory and I say this only to help someone who may have been trying to save someone from themself. It can only happen if they are willing to participate in their own salvation. There may come a day when you are not there to shield them from the consequences of their choices. It is not your fault. Over time, I realized that I am only responsible for my own choices and some things are just beyond my control. I hope you, my reader friend, are also able to arrive at this place of understanding and acceptance.

I gave myself the space to feel the depths of my grief, knowing that navigating this complex journey would require time and effort. And so, I adopted practices that became my lifelines, and I believe they may be valuable for others as they traverse the seasons of grief and loss.

I want to share these practices with you. I call them "practices" because they may not come naturally at first; they may require effort before becoming consistent or effortless. Together, let us take these first steps as we uncover the transformative power of healing and growing through grief.

Acknowledge the pain.

Every emotion serves a purpose, and pain is no exception. In the grieving process, pain lingers as a reminder of the love and affection we once bestowed upon someone who is no longer there to receive it. Pain fills the void left by their absence, and I like to think of it as the cost of loving deeply. It can be beneficial to allow yourself to experience this pain fully. Although it is uncomfortable, suppressing or avoiding pain in pursuit of immediate comfort or pleasure can be detrimental and hinder healing.

So, yes, allow the pain its rightful place in your heart. However, avoid allowing it to consume you entirely. One technique I found beneficial was allocating a specific time each day to sit with my emotions and be aware of them. During that time, I allowed myself to simply feel the pain without judgment or restraint. When the designated time was up, I gently reminded myself of other pressing matters that needed my attention. Even if I did not have anything important that required my immediate attention, I turned my thoughts elsewhere and my emotional state would soon return to normal. Sometimes, I would say to myself, "Ok, that's enough". The idea of simply turning off your emotions sounds weird and unnatural, but it worked for me. By doing so, I was able to function, honor my own needs and show up for the people who still depended on me. They became a big part of my "why", my reason to persevere. The other part was myself. Although it was still dark, I believed eventually light would show itself again. In the meantime, I permitted darkness to do the good work only it can do, as I worked through the literal and figurative fear of it. That is not to say that grief or loss is good, but I looked for the good that could come from it. During this period, I came across a Brian Weiner quote that says, "If you focus on the pain, you will continue to suffer. If you focus on the lesson, you will continue to grow." This resonated with me and so I incorporated a mission of learning, growing and improving as another part of my why.

What or whom is your "why"? If you are unsure, I encourage you to tap into a reason to continue, especially on the most difficult of days. Have you considered what lessons loss and pain may be trying to teach you, especially about yourself? Again, you may find it beneficial to seek useful, honest answers to these questions. Embracing the lessons and growth opportunities that only come through painful experiences can become a catalyst for healing and transformation. While you allow yourself the time and space for grief, hold on tightly to your why, perhaps discover your purpose and let it guide you towards hope and renewal. Also, remember you are not alone in this journey and there is strength in acknowledging your pain while continuing to press forward.

Identify your coping mechanisms.

Recognize that not everyone copes with grief in the same way. In other words, avoid comparing yourself to others. Instead, take a moment to reflect on your own coping strategies. Are they healthy or unhealthy? Your answer to this question will greatly impact how, and if, you navigate through the winter of grief, as well as how long your winter season may linger. Some examples of healthy coping mechanisms include journaling, exercise, listening to music or spending time in nature. These activities can provide solace and a sense of peace during difficult times.

Conversely, unhealthy coping mechanisms, such as excessive alcohol consumption, illicit drug use or engaging other risky behaviors may offer temporary relief from pain, but they also lead to additional problems, exacerbating the challenges you face instead of resolving them. Another way to symbolize unhealthy coping mechanisms is the game of whack-a-mole. The action may seem to suppress the pain in one way, but it invariably pops up somewhere else. When experiencing grief, suppression is not the goal. A more useful goal, in my view, is to move through grief at a healthy pace, which you decide. Over time, you can emerge, forever changed, but stronger, better, healed and whole.

I discovered I have two primary coping mechanisms: thought and activity. These would become the foundation of my healthy journey as I moved through grief's winter. During this period, I found myself in what I describe as a "loop", a recurring pattern of emotions, questions, then thoughts that produce calm. This loop consisted of internal dialogues, reasoning with myself, and encouraging myself with words of self-love and affirmation. Sometimes, these self-to-self discussions occurred silently in my mind. Other times, especially when I was alone or out for a walk, I would verbalize my positive thoughts to bring myself back to a space of calm. When something occurred to me that I thought would be useful to remember, I would write it on a sticky note and place it somewhere I could see it often. For me, this place was my bathroom. As I was starting my day, brushing my teeth, grooming myself, I drew strength from the inspirational and motivational messages I posted to my mirror on sticky notes. They were the constant reminders of the positive things about myself, my life, my husband, our relationship, as well as life in general, that I needed to sustain me in this cold, dreary season.

Through the process, utilizing the mechanisms that worked best for me, I found answers to some of the questions that mattered most. I also learned to accept that some questions may remain unanswered. The unknown can be frightening, but understanding my own limitations helped me to focus less on what was outside my control and more on the things I could do. Believe me when I say writing about it now is easier than it was to do it then. But it can be done. After a while, I knew where I was in the loop and what I had to do next to temporarily calm my mind and heart, with the hopes that the calm would linger longer as time passed, and it has. I encourage you to embrace the cyclical nature of grief. It doesn't always follow a linear path. This is why the same thoughts and emotions re-emerge until we are ready to move forward.

Engaging in various activities also played a significant role in helping me to cope. As someone who enjoys painting and decorating, I seized the opportunity to create projects in almost every room of the house, one at a time. Each one became a form of therapeutic release, though I understood that it could not replace professional therapy and I should note that I maintained weekly therapy sessions with a fantastic counselor during this period. In between sessions, painting, decorating and cleaning created a space in which I could think deeply or not think at all. Both were beneficial and I would go with it - except when I realized I was headed for a rabbit hole. That is what I call the succession of questions or thoughts that increase anxiety. At that point, I would call myself back to the present. And while tears were an integral part of my healing process (tears are good, let them flow), creating was a productive alternative that I looked forward to, and it was my way of taking back control over parts of my life. Through activity, I found peace during the day and a better night's sleep. What's more, over time, I noticed how my living space had transformed. This creative process helped me turn what was once our home into my sanctuary, enhancing my present moment and adding a touch of warmth to my surroundings. Do you have a productive activity that helps you cope?

In your own journey, explore the coping mechanisms that work best for you. Embrace the power of reflection, conversation and engaging in activities that bring you comfort and healing. Remember, healing is a multifaceted process, and it is entirely okay to seek help and find solace in various ways as you navigate the depths of grief. By acknowledging your coping mechanisms and embracing the cyclical nature of grief, you can pave the way for a meaningful journey of healing and growth. Have you noticed a theme emerging from each section so far? Yes, healing, growth and positive transformation are what I wish for you in your healing journey. It may sound odd that I keep referencing things like meaningfulness and growth. However, it is my belief that if suffering is going to visit, it might as well make itself useful.

Understand the grief process.

It is essential to recognize that grief encompasses both common and unique aspects. Not everyone will experience the common aspects of grief in the same order, and some may not encounter every component of the grieving process. Each person's grief journey is individual, and it is important to be gentle with yourself and avoid judging someone else's path, or even being overly critical of your own. It is ok to analyze and assess, but give yourself grace. If you are providing support to someone who is grieving, grace is key.

Remember that while profound sadness, anger, denial, and depression are common during grief's winter, you may also encounter a myriad of other emotions during this season.

I recall a moment in my kitchen, about a week after my husband's passing. I was surrounded by family who had come to offer support. I remember how despite being in the company of loved ones, I felt an overwhelming sense of pain and loneliness. Eating, something I normally enjoyed, was a chore, as guilt gnawed at me for still being alive when he was gone. Even as my sisters and others attempted to bring some lightheartedness to the situation with humor and by sharing fond memories, I found it hard to laugh without him.

Recall, my coping mechanisms are thought and action, so I had another candid internal conversation while standing at the stove. I told myself, "You must eat. You are still alive, and your body needs nourishment." With that, I fixed a small plate and ate. Afterwards, I joined in the laughter, relishing it, and knowing full well another wave of pain would soon come crashing in.

I want to delve deeper into the profound sense of loneliness that often accompanies this grief journey, for it is an emotion that will likely become a constant companion. Loneliness is a silent specter, stealthily creeping into the corners of your life when you least expect it. It's a companion that can turn even the most mundane tasks into overwhelming reminders of the absence of your life partner or loved one. Simple trips to the grocery store, once taken for granted, echo with a haunting emptiness. Aimless drives, which may have been leisurely escapes in the past feel vastly different, lacking the warmth of shared company.

The absence of those midday calls at work, filled with love and laughter, leaves an echoing void. For me, even the setting of the sun, which once marked the end of a day and the promise of a cozy evening together, triggered a profound sense of dread. Nighttime, when the world quiets down and shadows lengthen, can become the coldest and most isolating reminder of all. It's during these solitary hours that loneliness can wrap around you like a heavy shroud, making the ache of loss feel almost unbearable.

Loneliness in grief is not just the absence of someone you love; it's the absence of the shared moments, the familiar presence, and the deep connection that once helped define your life. It's a solitude that can seep into every corner of your existence, casting a long shadow over even the most routine activities. Recognizing and navigating this loneliness is an essential part of the healing process, as it allows you to acknowledge the depth of your emotions and take steps to find solace and connection, even in the midst of profound loss.

Now, having moved beyond the winter of my grief, I want to assure you that feeling your loved one's absence is entirely natural. You are not crazy. It makes sense if you feel as though parts of you are dying. That is the result of the profound connectedness you shared. In ways spiritual, emotional and physical, parts of you truly are affected.

I touched on this before, but I want to remind you that throughout this process, there will be portions of your journey that you must navigate alone – alone with your thoughts and feelings. However, it is critical to distinguish the feeling of loneliness and actually being isolated from your support system. Some people instinctively seek solitude and introspection during difficult times, and that is perfectly okay. However, be mindful of when necessary alone time transitions into harmful isolation which can hinder the healing process and exacerbate emotional struggles.

It is vital to understand what is expected and common during the grief process while also acknowledging what is normal for you personally. To help facilitate this understanding, consider connecting with a support group, seek counseling, and accept help from those who genuinely want to be there for you. Remember, healing is a multifaceted journey, and it's okay to seek guidance and companionship to help navigate the complexities of grief.

Embrace and practice self-care.

Have you ever considered how you care for your own needs? Do you pay attention to your emotional states and practice self-care? As adults, we often become adept at caring for others – our children, partners, and aging parents. However, amidst these responsibilities, we often forget to prioritize self-care. Taking time to meet our own needs is not selfish; it is an essential aspect of maintaining emotional well-being. Since it is true, you cannot pour from an empty cup, you must find ways to refill yours before it runs dry. Embracing this truth and practicing self-care can significantly impact how you navigate the challenges that life throws your way, especially during the winter of grief.

Let me reiterate: taking time for yourself is necessary, not selfish. Despite the weight of grief pressing upon your heart and thoughts, self-care is a crucial survival mechanism. Without it, you may find yourself overwhelmed and lost in your suffering.

As I share these practices with you, I want to remind you that grief's winter can feel like the longest, coldest, and most challenging season. Navigating through this dismal, often gloomy, season won't be easy, but equipping yourself with self-care practices can make it more manageable. While time may not completely heal all wounds (it is possible to remain in a perpetual state of healing), and winter may appear more than once in your journey, understanding that grief isn't always linear will help you gain perspective. Find your why during this season – the reasons to get out of bed, groom yourself, and avoid giving in to sadness. I didn't say don't feel sad. But if you always give in to it, it will overtake you. Feel it, but keep going, the way we often put aside our feelings, and even our health, for jobs that will quickly replace us. Remember, allow the darkness to serve its purpose as you equip yourself to persevere, knowing that life both takes and gives, and the strength to embrace each moment is within you.

From the list of self-care practices that follow, I encourage you to take those that resonate with you and adapt them to your unique needs and preferences.

Engage in enjoyable activities.
The grieving process is undeniably challenging, and during these times, seeking solace in activities that bring joy and respite can be invaluable. It's common to yearn for an escape from the overwhelming pain and emotions that accompany loss, and this is where engaging in healthy and beneficial activities comes into play. These activities can serve as a lifeline, providing moments of relief and a reprieve from the constant ache of grief.

For me, listening to music soothed my spirit. It always has. Music has a unique ability to touch our souls and evoke a wide range of emotions. However, in the early stages of grief, I found myself avoiding songs that my husband and I had once enjoyed together. The weight of those shared memories felt unbearable at the time. Instead, I turned to a different genre: jazz. The intricate melodies and wordless rhythms of jazz provided me with a sanctuary of sound where I could momentarily escape the pain.

When I would drive, I would immerse myself in the soothing, instrumental sounds of jazz music. The absence of lyrics allowed me to lose myself in the music's ebb and flow, providing a temporary respite from the constant tug of sorrow. It became a form of therapy, a way to release pent-up emotions without words, and a reminder that moments of peace were still possible, even in the midst of profound loss.

Engaging in activities that bring you joy, whether it's music, painting, hiking, or any other pursuit, can serve as a healing balm. These activities not only provide a distraction from the pain but also offer a means of self-expression and a connection to the world beyond grief. They serve as a reminder that life, in its entirety, is a complex tapestry of emotions, and even in the darkest moments, there are threads of joy to be found.

While it may seem challenging to embrace these activities initially, as grief can cast a long shadow, remember that they are a testament to your resilience. They are a way of honoring your loved one's memory by continuing to find joy and meaning in life. So, don't hesitate to seek solace in the activities that bring you comfort, for they hold the power to illuminate the path forward during the darkest of times.

Get active.
Incorporating physical activity into your routine can become a powerful tool for navigating the labyrinth of grief. It's important to understand that you don't need to set lofty fitness goals like running a marathon or becoming a weight-lifting champion. Instead, focus on selecting a form of exercise that genuinely brings you joy and meets you where you are in your grief journey.

Whether it's a leisurely walk, gentle yoga, swimming, or dancing to your favorite music, physical activity has the remarkable ability to act as an automatic mood-lifter. When we engage in these activities, our bodies release endorphins, often referred to as "feel-good" hormones, which can help alleviate some of the emotional pain that accompanies grief. These endorphins create a sense of well-being and, for a brief moment, offer respite from the heaviness of loss.

Additionally, spending time in nature can provide a refreshing and rejuvenating break from the confines of grief. Nature has a remarkable way of soothing the soul. When you're feeling low, consider setting a simple goal during a nature walk: identify five beautiful things in your surroundings. This could include gazing up at the expanse of the sky, admiring the intricate patterns of clouds, listening to the melodious songs of birds, or marveling at the grandeur of ancient trees.

This practice serves to shift your focus from the past and future, where grief often dwells, to the present moment. It encourages mindfulness—a conscious awareness of your immediate environment—and helps you appreciate the beauty and serenity that can be found even amidst life's storms.

By integrating physical activity and nature into your coping strategies, you're not attempting to erase your grief; rather, you're providing yourself with moments of relief and respite. These practices are like gentle companions, walking alongside you as you navigate the winding path of grief. They offer you a chance to breathe, to momentarily step out of the shadows, and to connect with the world around you.

Practice relaxation.
In the midst of grief's storm, finding moments of inner peace and tranquility can feel like an elusive dream. Yet, setting aside dedicated time to calm your heart and mind in a quiet, sacred space can become a vital lifeline. Here, you can retreat from the tumultuous waves of grief and begin to reconnect with your inner sanctuary.

Begin this practice by taking long, deliberate breaths. Feel yourself inhale and exhale, grounding you in the present moment. Deep breaths serve as an anchor, allowing you to momentarily detach from the weight of grief and regain a sense of balance.

As you settle into this space, focus your thoughts on something you have enjoyed in the past or envision something you'd like to do in the future. This act of reminiscing or daydreaming can transport you to a place of hope and joy, even if only for a brief moment. It's a reminder that there are still moments of happiness to be found, even when you are hurting.

If you find it challenging to quiet your thoughts or need additional guidance in achieving relaxation, consider exploring guided meditation. Guided meditation can be a gentle yet powerful tool in your healing toolkit. It offers you the opportunity to follow the soothing voice of a guide who leads you through a calming and centering meditation session.

I often listen to meditation music to chill out, unwind. The frequencies, melodies and gentle rhythms of this type of music create a serene backdrop for relaxation. Focusing on the music becomes a form of meditation in itself, allowing me to let go of the burdens of the day and drift into a state of peaceful contemplation. It's a practice that has served as a bridge to sleep during those restless nights when slumber seemed elusive.

Incorporating relaxation into your routine is not an attempt to erase grief or deny its existence; rather, it's a compassionate gesture to yourself. It's a recognition that, in all circumstances, you deserve moments of respite and self-care. These moments become your refuge, offering you the strength to face the tumultuous seas of grief with a centered and resilient spirit.

Ask for Help. Easy to say, but sometimes difficult to do, especially when you are in the throes of grief and pain. But when the weight of grief gets too heavy or becomes too much to bear alone, it is important to understand that it's not only acceptable but also commendable (and necessary) to reach out for help. Your vulnerability in seeking support is not a sign of weakness. On the contrary, it is an acknowledgment of your humanity and strength in facing the challenges that life has presented.

To facilitate healing, consider leaning on the pillars of support available to you. This support may come in various forms, from family and friends to grief counselors or therapists. Each one provides a unique source of comfort and guidance, offering you different perspectives and tools to help you navigate the complex terrain of grief.

Connecting with a support group can be especially beneficial. These groups are often individuals who have embarked on their own grief journeys and understand the grief-to-healing process. Their shared experiences can provide a sense of camaraderie and reassurance that you are not alone. It is within these circles that you may find kindred spirits who empathize with your sorrow and offer insights born from their own healing processes.

Mental health professionals, such as therapists or grief counselors, can bring a wealth of knowledge and expertise to your healing journey. They are skilled in helping you navigate the intricate layers of grief, providing you with tools and strategies to manage the emotional turbulence that accompanies loss. Their guidance can be transformative, helping you not only cope with grief but also embark on the path to creating a new chapter in your life.

I cannot emphasize enough that you are not alone in your grief. Seeking comfort and support from others is not only essential but also an act of self-care and self love. It is an acknowledgment that healing is not a solitary endeavor; it's a collective effort that draws strength from the love and compassion of those who care about you. By opening yourself to the support that surrounds you, you not only honor your own healing but also forge connections that can lead you toward the light of a new beginning, and potentially helping others.

Find ways to honor your loved one.
As you journey through the seasons of grief, you will discover that the memories of your loved one are both a source of solace and a bridge of connection. When you are ready and to the extent that feels comfortable, embracing these memories and actively finding ways to honor your loved one can be a powerful and healing experience.

Fondly remembering your loved one is a way of keeping their spirit alive in your heart. It is an acknowledgment that their presence, though physically absent, continues to influence your life. These memories become the threads that weave a tapestry of their enduring impact on your journey.

Cherishing shared memories is a tender act of gratitude which allows you to relive moments of joy, love, and laughter that you once shared. These recollections are like precious gems that you can hold close to your heart, a reminder that the bond you shared transcends the boundaries of time and space.

Carrying on your loved one's legacy is a way of ensuring their light continues to shine in the world. It is a commitment to embody the values, wisdom, and love they imparted to you. This legacy becomes a torch that you carry forward, illuminating your path and the paths of others you encounter.

Creating a memorial is a tangible expression of your love and respect. It can take various forms, allowing you to choose a gesture that resonates with your heart, or perhaps your loved one's wishes. Some choose to establish a physical space, like a garden or a bench, dedicated to their loved one's memory. This space can become a sanctuary where you can retreat to reflect, find comfort, and feel the enduring presence of your loved one.

Lighting a candle is a simple yet profoundly symbolic act. It represents the eternal flame of love that burns brightly within you. The flickering light becomes a beacon of hope and remembrance, casting a warm glow that dispels the darkness of grief.

Releasing balloons is a gesture that offers a feeling of liberation and connection. As the balloons ascend into the sky, it's as though you are sending your love and messages to your loved one in the heavens. The act of letting go can be therapeutic, allowing you to release pent-up emotions and find a sense of peace.

Ultimately, finding ways to honor your loved one is a deeply personal and intimate journey. It is a testament to the enduring bond that transcends physical existence. It's a celebration of the love and memories that continue to shape your life. And, most importantly, it's a way of keeping their presence alive in your heart, providing comfort and peace as you look toward the next chapters of your life.

Pray or Connect to Your Source. In the intricate tapestry of grief, finding solace and strength often involves a spiritual or transcendental dimension. For many, prayer is a deeply meaningful and comforting practice that provides a channel to connect with their source of faith, whether it be a higher power, the universe, or a divine presence.

When you turn to prayer, you open a sacred dialogue with your source. It is a place where you can pour out your heart and soul, sharing your deepest fears, pain, and vulnerabilities. In these moments, you are assured you are not alone. You are embraced by the unconditional love and compassion of your source.

As you articulate your pain and anguish, you release the weight of grief that may have been suffocating your spirit. This release is like unburdening of your soul, allowing you to breathe more freely and feel the gentle embrace of comfort and assurance.

In prayer, you can ask for strength to face the challenges that lie ahead. It is an affirmation of your resilience and an acknowledgment that, even in the darkest moments, you have the inner fortitude to endure. This request for strength is a testament to your belief in your ability to navigate the intricate terrain of grief and emerge stronger on the other side.

Each moment of prayer becomes a sanctuary of hope and an opportunity to express gratitude. It's a place where you can find peace in the midst of chaos, clarity in the depths of confusion, and peace amid the turbulence of emotions. It is a reminder that, no matter how overwhelming the grief may seem, you are held in the loving embrace of your source.

Whether your prayer is whispered in the quiet of your heart, spoken aloud, or written in a journal, it carries a sacred energy that can provide immeasurable comfort and healing. It's an anchor that helps you navigate the shifting tides of grief, offering you a sense of purpose and a reminder that you are never alone on this journey.

Ultimately, prayer or connection to your source is a deeply personal and intimate practice. It's a pathway to finding solace, comfort, and healing as you navigate the seasons of grief, reminding you that there is a source of strength and love that walks beside you every step of the way.

Remember, these are merely suggestions, and what matters most is finding what works for you. The goal is to neither rush nor prolong the grief process, but to understand that prolonged stress can weaken the body's defenses over time. Self-care offers relief from stress and pain, allowing you to focus on the present moment, where life is actually happening; not in the suffering of yesterday or your anxiety about tomorrow. It also helps you prioritize taking care of your own needs. When your focus has been taking care of others or in the absence of an attentive significant other, putting yourself first can be a challenge or even feel unnatural. I assure you, self-care is normal, if not natural, as well as necessary.

Navigating through this dreary season is crucial, and equipping yourself with self-care practices can make it more manageable. While time may not heal all wounds, and winter may appear more than once in your journey, understanding that grief isn't always linear will help you gain perspective. Find your why during this season – the reasons to get out of bed, groom yourself, and avoid giving in to sadness. Equip yourself to persevere, knowing that life both takes and gives, and the strength to embrace each moment is within you.

Speaking of give and take, it was during the winter of my grief that my first grandchild was born. She arrived two months early, and as expected, our lives were filled with special and challenging moments in and out of the hospital as she spent her first month of life in the NICU. This new addition to our family quickly transported me back into the present. Despite the damp, dim winter days (as we were entering the holiday season) and continued long nights, her beautiful little eyes and hands, all of her, weighing just four pounds, captivated me. She was released from the hospital a week before Christmas. With her arrival came someone who needed all the love I had inside, and I gladly showered her with it. And there it was, joy in the midst of sorrow! Life has a way of giving us gifts when we least expect but need them most. If you believe life has given you nothing, I encourage you to look again. If you don't find something or someone, know it is on the way.

As you find yourself able to embrace new joy while grieving, remember that the new is not intended to replace what was lost. What is no more was a part of your yesterday. What has come is part of your present. I touched on this earlier, and I know it may seem difficult to believe, but winter doesn't just come to bring pain; it can also be the season during which your purpose is born. Embrace the season, know that it is temporary, and learn the lessons that it teaches as you heal, grow and transform. I am certain it is what your loved one would want for you, and it's what I want for you, too. Remember, you are a soul survivor, bent but not broken. Everything you need to make it through the winters of your life is either already within you or waiting for you to discover it.

As you continue our voyage together in the pages of this book, keep in mind the practices I have shared can be applied and add value during each season of your process. I challenge you to begin today embracing self-care – rest, meditate, pray (if that is something you do), and find a reason to keep going.

Allow these and other helpful practices to fill your cup with peace, joy, love, wisdom, and strength. And if something that once served you loses its usefulness, feel free to adapt or replace it with a new practice that nurtures your soul. Remember, it's okay to evolve and change. You are going to be okay. You are going to be whole again. Let us embrace this truth together.

Winter's Words

In the pages that follow, I encourage you to take some time to journal your thoughts and feelings during this season. Writing your thoughts is a form of therapeutic release. You may find it useful to periodically review your entries to determine how far you have traveled in your grief and healing journey.

Let's unpack. What have been the predominant emotions of this season?

_____

_____

_____

_____

_____

Have you set aside time for stillness and introspection? What do you think about during those times?

_____

_____

_____

_____

_____

Have you practiced self-care? If so, in what way(s)?

_____

_____

_____

What are you hoping to remember or forget about your winter grief season?

_____
_____
_____
_____
_____
_____
_____
_____
_____
_____

Have you learned something new about yourself?

_____
_____
_____
_____
_____
_____
_____
_____

Please use the additional space to practice journaling. You can include thoughts, feelings, memories, goals. This is your healing space.

_____

_____

_____

_____

_____

_____

_____

_____

_____

_____

_____

_____

_____

_____

_____

_____

_____

_____

In the depths of sorrow's night,
Resilience finds its growing light.
Through tears that fall, we learn to rise,
As darkness subsides, a new sunrise.

Grief's storm may rage, its painful winds blow,
What once felt like breaking,
In time, makes us grow.
As we face each new challenge, we are remade,
We blossom, then bloom, changed yet unafraid.

FALL

A couple things come to mind when I think about fall in the context of grief. First, not everyone experiences this season, such as instances of sudden, unexpected loss. But for those who do, as with our natural seasons, this metaphorical season precedes winter. The cool air is a constant reminder that winter is on its way. Trees begin to shed their foliage and the days grow shorter. This vision of fall reminds me of a loved one who has been diagnosed with a terminal illness or a loved one who has been battling with illness for an extended period. We watch helplessly as our loved one experiences changes to their physical appearance, acuity, demeanor and sometimes, their will to survive. We try to balance making the most of the time that remains while preparing ourselves for what is to come.

I have encountered powerful, transformational fall grief experiences, two of which occurred within 1-3 years of my husband's passing. The first was with an aunt who was very dear, helped raise me and, in my adult life, she became a cherished friend. She had been a staple in my life, all my life. We shared more laughs over the years than I can count and shed a few tears, too. I remember how we'd call each other and literally talk for hours. She provided a listening ear, a supportive shoulder, words of encouragement and caution, as well as wise counsel. Aunt Elizabeth had an outgoing personality and a huge laugh that seemed to emanate from her soul. I am so grateful to have known her and appreciate the gifts she shared with me; some to hold, and others to pass on to others.

Before she was diagnosed with dementia, it seemed to us, the family, that she was experiencing a deep depression. She was sometimes withdrawn and sad. We knew something was wrong. It wasn't until I was in grad school as a psychology major that I learned dementia sometimes presents as depression. In the years that followed her diagnosis, I watched as her personality and physical appearance changed. Her condition worsened to the point that, by the time she reached her final months, little of the person I had known and loved remained. It was during the height of the pandemic that she suffered an injury in the nursing home which triggered the beginning of multiple hospital stays. It was also during this period that difficult discussions and even more difficult decisions had to be made, as the doctors' reports created a clear narrative of her prognosis. Like fall, constant, sometimes rapid change became the norm. Once her condition deteriorated to the point that medical intervention became ineffective, my aunt was transported to hospice where she had one final birthday and, although she had lost the ability to speak, she was able to see the last of her grandchildren, born 11 days before her passing, via FaceTime. It was the epitome of the bittersweet nature of the cycle of life.

When we received the call that she likely had only hours remaining, some of the family came to her bedside and stayed through the night, talking and praying. We left in the morning with intentions of returning. However, it seemed she waited until she was alone to breathe her last. I remember going to the grocery store to pick up some items when I got a call from home. I didn't answer the first call. I was not ready for the words I knew I was about to hear. Of course, the second call came immediately after the first. I answered and, hearing the cries and screams of my family on the other end of the line, I prepared myself to support them. I too was sad, hurt and grieving, but what helped me through it was the close relationship I had with her. I knew she was gone and I missed her, but I knew her so well that I felt I could almost hear her response to any question I might ask, her response to whatever I might say. Her laugh still rings in my ears and, because she had not been herself for so long, I realized I had begun grieving for her long before she passed away.

I also had a revelation that wasn't new or surprising, but the truth of it simplified my thoughts and feelings. Here on earth, three things are happening. People are entering into this life, while others are in the process of living. Still others are in the process of dying. That's the deal. And at the appointed times, we mourn the loss of others until it is our turn to be mourned. That truth struck me as a fact more easily understood than accepted, but it stayed with me and prevented me from asking questions and seeking answers that, even if discovered, would not return her to life.

We have talked about the falling leaves, rapid changes and shorter, less-sunny days as a prelude to winter. However, as with the other seasons, there is beauty in fall. I am reminded of this when I recall my visits with my aunt at my home and in the nursing home, combing her hair, telling her the latest news (and by news, I mean tea). She loved some hot tea! Sometimes, I would embellish a bit just to get her to laugh. While they weren't the large, from-the-belly laughs we used to enjoy together, they were just as special, if not moreso. In other words, while I was aware that winter would come, I made a conscious effort to enjoy every moment I could in the present. One time, while we were listening to music she enjoyed in her younger days, a Luther Vandross song came on. I said, teasing her, "That's your man, auntie!" She responded emphatically, and with a little attitude, "He used to be." I could hardly get out the words "Well, alrighty then" for laughing. That was the best laugh of my day, and she had a good chuckle too. It was a moment I shared with the aunt I knew so well and, I believe, a moment of clarity for her. I will always remember that.

I encourage you, if you are in the midst of a fall season, try not to allow sadness to be all you take with you into the seasons ahead. Instead, muster all the joy and good memories you can. Someday, they may comfort you and, in the moment, they may be a vital source of joy to your loved one who could be struggling internally (or out loud) to make sense of or find peace in their final chapters.

A year after my aunt's passing, I had another fall grief experience with my father. Just to share a bit about my daddy, he had the best sense of humor of anyone I have ever known. He was hilarious and a character! He would say things about people, things and situations that could only emanate from his mind and mouth. He had a beautiful singing voice and he loved music, which he passed on to me (not the beautiful singing voice, just the love of music). He was a good cook and great on the grill. He took pride in passing on his skills to the younger men in the family. Two scenes into a movie, he was able to accurately predict who did what. And although he also battled with depression that often presented as pessimism, Daddy had an interesting, unique perspective and could share deep insights about life and people. He was outspoken and called balls and strikes, often without invitation. He did not need permission to speak his truth. We had a very close relationship, which he once referred to as our "journey". We could talk about practically anything, and we did.

In September 2021, my father was diagnosed with stage four, small-cell lung cancer. He had been coughing for months and I thought maybe he had a respiratory infection. He thought he may have developed emphysema, as he was a four-decades-long smoker. We had just buried his sister, who I referenced above, the year before, along with the two remaining family matriarchs. And just when he was beginning to come to visit again as he had completely isolated himself during COVID. A cancer diagnosis. We were both taken completely by surprise. I suppose we were both looking forward to rebuilding life after COVID. Instead, I watched as my father geared up for the battle of a lifetime; the final battle of his lifetime.

Damn.

I believe it was late August when my daughter had taken daddy to the emergency room. He wasn't feeling well and said he needed to go right away and she was closer at the time. I came after he had been checked into a room. I was with him when the ER doctor came in after viewing x-rays of his lungs. She told him, matter-of-factly, that his left lung was completely white and her guess was it was cancer. In the ER! Her guess?! I could not believe the callousness or the willingness to, without solicitation, offer up a diagnosis. I looked away from her. I didn't even want to see her. My gaze fell on my father to see if her words landed on him with the same weight I was feeling. Neither his tone nor his facial expression changed. He continued as if she had not just delivered potentially life-altering news. I asked him later how he was feeling, trying to match his tone and not react to the news or its delivery. He simply said, "I will find out when I follow up with my doctor."

I recall taking him to an imaging center in late September. By then, he had an oncologist and we were preparing for chemo. Sitting in the car, I called one of my sisters. When she answered, I said, "There isn't much time." I was open to a miracle. I would have been completely ecstatic to hear the cancer was in remission or completely gone. But, because it was late-stage, I knew it was going to be an uphill climb with little hope of reaching the top.

Looking back, I am grateful for the way we shared our time. I remember him calling me in April to ask me if I was planning to throw him a birthday party because he wanted to invite some of his friends from St. Augustine. Did I mention he was a character? I told him I wasn't planning to do anything big. I had thrown him a big to-do for his 65th birthday and planned to do another large celebration for his 70th. I mentioned his request to his oldest sister. She replied, "Throw him a party." So I did. I'm so glad I did not wait for a birthday he would never see to celebrate him.

Daddy came to live with me once he was diagnosed. The family made sure Thanksgiving and Christmas were special. Lifelong friends and family he hadn't seen in many years called and visited. We watched his favorite movie during Christmas, *It's a Wonderful Life*. I held it together during the movie, then cried later, when I was alone. It was a tradition and I feared it would be the last time we would see it together. We made sure he had the things he enjoyed, and created memories in the home. Chemo left him too drained to venture out of the house. My son would play the theme song to Rocky IV as he left for his treatments, which made him smile. I recall how he loved spending time with his only great-grand. Their connection was kismet. He lit up when I brought her into his room and when he spoke to her, calling her "grandpapa's baby", she always giggled and spoke back in a language that, as an infant, only she understood. We just knew she seemed to love her grandpa-pa. That meant everything to him.

In the midst of all that I just described, my father continued to lose weight rapidly and he struggled to catch his breath after taking a few steps. His appetite dwindled. About a week after Christmas on the heels of months of chemo and immunotherapy came the news we didn't want to hear. The mass had grown. Then, even more bad news; my father decided not to pursue additional treatment options and his doctor agreed with his choice. There were no other options.

This was one helluva metaphorical fall in the middle of natural winter.

During daddy's final visit with the oncologist, it was estimated he had 1-3 months remaining. Hospice was called into our home. Still, I was responsible for administering morphine and my son helped with his care. I mention this because it was the only aspect of caring for him that I hated to do. I understood that it kept his pain at bay, but I was uncomfortable with being a part of his dying process in that way. My daughter was there, too, but I think it was either too much for her or perhaps it was surreal. After all, we had already seen so much loss. One day, I believe I was out and my father asked my daughter to wheel him into the front room. She began to play music he enjoyed and it lifted his spirit. She sometimes still talks about how happy they both were that day. Daddy opened his arms wide to embrace her, his first grandchild, as we were leaving the hospice facility the night before he passed. He was moved to a hospice facility 4 days before his passing, which occurred about 3 weeks after the final oncologist visit.

On the way home from the doctor's office, daddy and I stopped to pick up a prescription. As we waited in the drive-thru line, he turned to me and thanked me for "the journey". We said what we needed and wanted to say. He called the family together to discuss his prognosis and share his decision. He said, "Death is coming and it's already here." There's an example of that perspective that I told you about. Some of us were in the room and others were on the phone. Everyone expressed their love. As sad as it was, there was joy in knowing he was able to experience the love of his family as he prepared himself for what was unknown to him. Outwardly, he said, "This isn't my home anyway." Inwardly, I am sure there was turmoil.

His brother flew in from Delaware. His sister came and stayed. His nephews and niece came to visit. Old lovers called to reminisce and say farewell. He had only daughters and we all expressed our love. He was surrounded by so much love as he accepted his own mortality. I hope it made what my son called the most bitter of pills the tiniest bit easier to swallow. And although I wanted more time, I was grateful for sharing 50 years of his life.

Two hours before he went away, I received a call. It was about 6:30 am on a Sunday. As soon as I heard the phone ring, my heart raced. I knew who it was and what the call was about before I looked at the phone. I answered to receive the news I had grown weary of hearing. Then I told my daughter where I was going, but I drove to the facility alone. I knew time was not waiting for me and I had no desire to wait for anyone else. My only concern was getting to his bedside. As daddy journeyed past this life, I went back as far as I could remember and thanked him while playing his favorite gospel songs until he breathed his last. His niece, granddaughter and great-granddaughter were also there, praying and bidding farewell when he drew his final breath.

Clearly, this was a fall grief experience that included all the elements of the season; falling leaves, changing temperatures and lots of rapid change. Remember, your experience may not be like mine. I have shared my experiences to illustrate that you are not alone, and in the hopes that there may be something in my fall seasons you find relatable or useful.

I realize I did not mention the part where I broke down. As a person who is more comfortable thinking than feeling, I mainly held it together. When my father passed, I had already written his obituary, made arrangements with the funeral home, picked out the suit he would wear, cleaned his apartment, and I believe I had started creating the programs for the funeral. I did not know what to expect from myself after his passing, so I took care of as much as possible while he was here so I would have the space to grieve when the time came, without the added burden of a thousand decisions to make. I think having already experienced so much loss in a short period made me more, not less, equipped to manage this extremely difficult loss. Still, I am by no means trivializing the experience. The death of my father hit differently than any other loss. Winter indeed revisited. The most painful and challenging aspects entailed navigating all the "firsts" without him – the first birthday, the first holiday season, all moments where his presence was deeply missed. Those first holidays were more painful than any others I recall. That's when the tears flowed and my heart ached. I really had to rely on my toolkit, family and my faith to stay afloat.

Earlier, when discussing coping tools, I emphasized the importance of honoring your loved one. I firmly believe that my dad would want me to live life to the fullest, embracing joy and moving forward despite the void his absence created. In doing so, I find comfort in imagining that he would be pleased if he could see me now. He would want me to be strong and resilient, but real. That is also what I wanted, and continue to strive to be. Again, I say, if this is not where you are, it is ok. It's ok if you break down. It's ok if you don't have all the details planned out. It's ok if you prefer to feel without thinking so much. Remember, there is no one way to process grief and your primary obligation is to embark on your own healing journey as your grieve, caring for your own needs along the way.

Nowadays, to honor my dad's memory, I try to keep his spirit alive in various ways. I often talk about him, sharing our cherished memories with family and friends. Now, I have shared some of our special memories with you. He would love that. To celebrate his humor and unique personality, I had some of his funniest sayings printed on t-shirts, reminding me of the laughter we shared. I reflect on the best times we had together, cherishing those precious moments. Most importantly, I pray for his eternal peace and believe he is free from the suffering he endured in this life.

So, how can you get through your fall? You can draw upon the same coping practices we used during winter. As the leaves of your grief journey gently or rapidly begin to change color, it is important to acknowledge the unique challenges that the fall season brings. This is a time of reflection and letting go, much like the leaves falling from the trees, making space for new growth in the seasons ahead.

Additionally, it is essential to recognize that if you are caring for a parent, spouse, child, or another loved one during this period, incorporating self-care and building a supportive network are vital aspects of your journey. Just as the trees prepare to weather the colder months by shedding their leaves, you too need to shed any notions that self-care is selfish, unnecessary or impossible. It is an essential part of being able to support and care for your loved one effectively. Just as you care for them, remember to care for yourself. Nurture your physical and emotional well-being, finding solace in simple activities that replenish your spirit.

By creating a network of support, whether through friends, family, community resources, or counseling, you can find comfort in knowing that you don't have to carry the burden alone. Much like the intertwined branches of the trees in a forest, the strength of your support network can provide stability and reassurance during these challenging times. Sharing your feelings, fears, and hopes with others who understand and empathize can provide a much-needed source of strength.

During this time, I also encourage you to embrace every opportunity to honor your loved one by sharing cherished memories and creating new ones together. Just as the fall season is a time of transition, it's also an opportunity to celebrate the life that was and the moments that are. Gather with loved ones to reminisce, laugh, and remember the beauty that your loved one brought into your life. By focusing on the positive memories, you can infuse this season with a sense of gratitude and warmth that can help carry you through the colder days.

I am reminded of how my aunt Elizabeth's wise words ring true; "Do what you can and accept that after you've done all you can, there's nothing else to do." It is during these moments of acceptance that the wisdom of the fall season truly shines. Just as the trees surrender their leaves to the ground, there comes a time to surrender to the reality that some aspects of life in general, as well as our specific circumstances, are beyond our control. Accepting this truth can help prevent unnecessary stress, guilt, and pain. By finding the balance between embracing the present, putting what has passed into perspective and accepting what you cannot change, you can navigate your fall season with resilience and hope.

Fall Fruits

Let's reflect on fall and continue to practice release and healing through journaling.

Time to unpack. What have been the predominant emotions of this season? What differences have you noticed between fall and winter? Keep in mind, there is no set order in which to experience the seasons, and you may not experience every season. Write what is applicable to your unique experience.

_____

_____

_____

_____

_____

_____

What memories or aspects of your grief journey do you find yourself holding on to?

_____

_____

_____

_____

_____

In what ways have you practiced self-compassion to allow yourself to release burdens that no longer serve you?

_____

_____

_____

_____

_____

_____

Please use the remaining space to document aspects of your fall grief season that have been impactful or transformative, or simply write what comes to mind.

_____

_____

_____

_____

_____

_____

_____

Beneath the weight of sorrow's shroud,
In spring's embrace, a whisper loud.
A bud of hope, a gentle call,
In grief's own time, we stand up tall.

New life emerges, tender and bright,
Breaking through the veil of night.
With each new bloom, a step ahead,
Resilient spirit, gently led.

SPRING

When spring graces the natural world, it brings a magical transformation. I envision the warming sun, gently caressing the earth, thawing the remnants of winter's chill. The days grow longer, stretching their arms to embrace the newfound warmth. As I step outside, I imagine I am greeted by the sweet aroma of blooming flowers, a symphony of colors that paint the landscape. The air is filled with the delightful scent of fresh-cut grass, evoking memories of carefree afternoons spent outdoors.

In this season of renewal, life bursts forth in abundance. Nature's canvas is adorned with delicate buds, with the promise of vibrant blossoms soon to unfurl. Everywhere I look, there are signs of life awakening from its slumber. Ponds come alive with baby ducks, gracefully gliding on the water, while the melodies of birds fill the early morning air. In my backyard, fawns venture out, their innocent eyes curious about the world they are just beginning to explore. The once barren landscape is transforming into a lush green carpet, inviting life to flourish once more.

Grief's spring, in reality, might not match the grandeur of my idealized image of the physical season. Although my recollections of my spring grief season are not specific, I distinctly recall the weight of sorrow gradually lifting, like a fog dissipating in the morning light. The tears came less frequently, and the burden of guilt and sadness gradually gave way to a sense of acceptance. A newfound hope began to emerge, coaxing me to shift my focus from dwelling on the past to embracing the possibilities of the future.

During this transformative phase, I came to a profound realization: life would continue its relentless march forward, regardless of whether I actively participated in it or not. I understood that remaining in a perpetual state of grief, as if it were a tribute to those I had lost, held no genuine value for anyone, including myself. Instead, it hindered my ability to move forward and find a semblance of contentment. Choosing joy became a deliberate act, a conscious effort to embrace the moments of happiness that life offered. It wasn't an attempt to dismiss the significance of my loss, but rather a commitment to honor my own well-being and the memory of my loved ones by finding purpose and fulfillment in the present.

From time to time, I would remind myself that my father lost his father as a teenager and buried his mother at the age of 26. He would then journey more than 40 years with only the memories they shared during his early years, but it is the cycle of life. I could see him in my mind's eye, singing his mother's favorite gospel song from his soul. He was a young man then and I was a little girl. I remembered the times he became emotional reminiscing about his parents long after I became an adult. Suddenly, in my reflections, I gained a different understanding of his pain….because I knew it. And I became even more grateful for the time we shared, recognizing that he was with me for many more years than he had with his parents. I also accepted that it was my turn to journey on without him physically, but forever in my heart; our memories alive and completely accessible anytime I needed or wanted to recall.

That was my spring of grief experience. Yours may look completely different, and that is completely understandable and acceptable. Meanwhile, I have more to share with you about this season.

My goal in sharing imagery of spring is to, of course, mirror the journey of grief, as well as offer you something beautiful as a possibility of what awaits, not to define your season. As I previously mentioned, during the winter of grief, parts of oneself may feel as though they are withering away. But just as the natural world experiences a rebirth in spring, so too does the human spirit. Spring offers a glimmer of hope, reminding us that life is a continuous cycle of renewal and growth. I believe, over time, like the budding flowers and baby animals, we too are given the opportunity to awaken to a new chapter in our lives.

How does the thought of renewal and starting a new chapter make you feel right now?

Aside from hope and renewal, other markings of spring include a shift in how you are affected by cherished memories of your loved one. During spring these can become a source of comfort rather than overwhelming sorrow. I encourage you to embrace your memories and, if it helps, consider writing them down in a journal. Documenting your feelings and thoughts can also provide valuable insights into your healing journey and how far you've come since the depths of winter.

It is crucial to understand that moving forward and letting go of pain does not equate to forgetting your loved one. For some, pain becomes a tether that keeps them connected to their deceased family member. For others, the fear of leaving pain behind arises from uncertainty about what lies on the other side. I, too, experienced this struggle concerning my husband and had to grant myself permission to embrace happiness, growth, and the unknown.

During spring, the time that was once dedicated solely to grieving now shifts toward self-improvement and making plans for the future. I encourage you to set meaningful, incremental goals for yourself across various aspects of life, whether they be professional, spiritual, or related to your physical well-being. Widows and widowers, for example, may contemplate the possibility of companionship as they enter grief's spring, which is a natural part of the healing process.

Writing down your goals and revisiting them daily can help you stay focused and motivated. Regularly assess your progress and adjust your goals or behavior as needed. It is important to remember that the metaphorical seasons of grief are not confined to specific timelines like those in the natural world. The journey through grief is unique to each individual and may take months, years, or even fluctuate between different seasons. If you find yourself transitioning back to a previous phase, consider seeking support to cope with challenges and understand the underlying reasons. Avoid rushing the process, and allow yourself to sit with your emotions and experiences.

By now, I have repeatedly stated, grief is deeply personal, and there is no one-size-fits-all approach. Learn what works best for you, and be mindful of thoughts and behaviors that promote healing and well-being. Surround yourself with a supportive network of friends, family, or professionals who can offer comfort and guidance throughout this transformative journey. Remember, Spring is a season of hope and growth. And as you continue to honor your loved one's memory and yourself, embrace the opportunity for new beginnings and a future filled with promise.

Spring Song

I realize that not every song is sweet, or joyous and grief's spring can be a season of sweet-bitterness. What are the words to your spring song? They don't have to rhyme. They only need to reflect how you feel.

_____

_____

_____

_____

_____

_____

_____

_____

_____

_____

_____

What aspects of your life do you believe are ready for renewal and growth?

_____

_____

_____

_____

_____

What small steps can you take to embrace new beginnings and opportunities in your life?

_____

_____

_____

_____

_____

How do you envision your personal journey of healing and renewal in the coming months?

_____

_____

_____

_____

Write your thoughts and feelings about your spring grief and healing experience. In what ways are you different? What lessons have you learned? What have you discovered that gives you hope?

_____

_____

_____

_____

_____

_____

_____

_____

_____

_____

In the summer sun, we find our way,
Grief's shadows fade, with each passing day.
Love's memories serve as a guiding light,
Toward life in the present, and a future bright.

As we embrace joy amidst the pain,
Life's song continues its sweet refrain.
With open hearts and spirits free,
We learn to live, to love, to be.

SUMMER

What I love most about summer are the long, sunlit days that bring a surge of energy and productivity. It's a season filled with warmth, vibrant activities, and cherished gatherings like family reunions, graduations, parties, and vacations. Except for the sweltering Florida heat, I adore everything about summer.

Unlike our natural summer, there isn't much to love about grief, but perhaps one can be grateful for the profound changes it can bring and the potential for a beautiful new life and stronger self that could await on the other side. I view the summer of grief as a time when you may start to feel a semblance of yourself again. In this season, you have become adept at using coping mechanisms and other tools to improve your world, and life starts to regain its luster.

Just as the summer sun casts its glow across the landscape, illuminating even the darkest corners, the memories and presence of our departed loved ones stay with us. The ache of not having them to share life might still linger occasionally, but acceptance begins to bloom in this summer of grief. Life continues in full swing, and as we flow with it, we find moments of peace and contentment.

This season invites us to explore refined coping mechanisms, tools that have proven to be effective in navigating the complex terrain of grief. It's the time to engage in practices that provide solace and support, such as journaling, meditation, or seeking professional guidance. These tools, like rays of sunlight filtering through the trees, help illuminate the path forward and offer a sense of direction.

For instance, these days, when I think of my father, joy and laughter fill my heart. Though he is no longer here, his essence lives on within me. His DNA courses through my veins, and in the mirror, sometimes I glimpse his features in my own reflection. I cherish the legacy he left behind, and pass on his wisdom to his grandchildren to ensure his memory endures through generations. In my heart and mind, our bond transcends time and is immune to death. This perspective stands as a tribute to the unbreakable ties of love and memory.

However, the journey through grief is not without its complexities and challenges. The variations in how we experience loss are as diverse as the colors of a summer sunset. This is evident in my perspective concerning my husband's death. The complexities of suicide have made the grieving process intricate and, at times, agonizing. Unlike the fond memories I hold of my father and aunt, my husband's death has left a scar on my heart. Now and then, the wound reopens, and the pain returns. It is almost impossible for me to reminisce on how we began without remembering how it all ended, or to think about the good times we shared apart from the events of his final day of life. Like you, I am still on grief's journey, as well as life's journey and perhaps this, too, will change in time.

Nevertheless, amidst the complexities, challenges, and fluctuating seasons, I accept the reality of then and now, reclaim my joy when I feel it slipping away, simplify my thoughts, and ground myself in the present. Our entire story will forever be a part of my own and I loved him, but I still have more chapters to write. His life was meaningful to me, and if I could have chosen, I'd have written a different ending for him, one preceded by a life long and well-lived. Ultimately, the choice was not mine to make. I can and do disagree with his decision, but I cannot change it.

Thankfully, my power and hope lies not in what is outside my control, but in things I can do. And so does yours. Hence, this letter I have written to you. I hope you have found the words contained in the pages of this book useful, motivating and inspiring. I hope the aspects of our shared grief experience to which you can relate serve as reminders that you are not alone. I also hope that you will embrace the feelings and experiences that make your grief and healing journey unique.

May you find strength and purpose in your journey as you learn to accept the thorn is a necessary component of the rose and grief is an inextricable element of the human experience. This season also beckons you to explore a sense of purpose amidst the challenges. Engaging in meaningful activities, supporting others, or pursuing personal goals can provide an anchor during times of uncertainty. These actions can serve as the soil in which your growth takes root, blossoming in unexpected and beautiful ways.

Perhaps one day you, too, will share your story, allowing it to serve as someone else's inspiration as well as your personal reminder that there is life after loss. Remember, just as summer's warmth brings life to nature, your journey through grief can nurture the growth of your inner strength and resilience.

Summer Solace

What are the positive characteristics and strengths you have discovered within yourself during your grief and healing journey?

_____

_____

_____

_____

_____

_____

_____

How have you found moments of joy during difficult times?

_____

_____

_____

_____

_____

What activities or practices bring you a sense of fulfillment or help you
connect peacefully to the world around you?

_____

_____

_____

_____

_____

_____

_____

What changes have taken place in you since grief's winter and what are
you looking forward to now that you weren't before?

_____

_____

_____

_____

_____

_____

Seasons of Change: Navigating

Various Forms of Loss

As we have embarked on our journey through the seasons of grief, we've delved into the intricate tapestry of emotions that accompany the profound loss of a loved one. But the truth is, life is a journey punctuated by numerous forms of loss, each carrying its own unique impact and transformative potential. In this chapter, we'll broaden our exploration to briefly encompass diverse experiences of loss—spanning from the dissolution of a marriage to the fading of dreams and the complexities of family discord. Just as the seasons shape the world around us, these distinct forms of loss can mold and influence our path as well.

What we've gleaned from the preceding chapters is that even the most bitter pills can serve as powerful medicine, a healing catalyst. We can harness the most challenging circumstances for growth, learning to relinquish control over what's beyond our grasp and embracing gratitude, even when it seems scarce.

Gratitude is a powerful force that significantly influences, if not dictates, the quality of all life's seasons. It redirects our focus from what's lost to what remains—a celebration of what and who we still hold dear. While some circumstances are beyond our control and irreversible, our thoughts remain within our domain. Thoughts shape emotions, which in turn guide behaviors. Gratitude becomes a compass leading us to higher ground, a wellspring of comfort in the valleys of life. It's important to note that embracing gratitude doesn't equate to suppressing grief. Grief, in its varied forms, is an essential part of our journey, and it deserves its time and space.

Consider the example of divorce, a season akin to the harshness of winter. It ushers in a unique isolation and emptiness, reminiscent of the barren landscape. Divorce marks a period in which significant relationships fade or change, casting an aura of uncertainty over the future. In many ways, divorce can be likened to a form of death—the death of love, bonds, and dreams for shared tomorrows. As winter prompts us to seek warmth, divorce calls upon us to seek solace among friends, family, and professionals. Healing requires time, the opportunity to rebuild, and the groundwork for a new beginning. Similar to grief over a loved one's passing, the journey through divorce is unique for each individual. The process may span months or even years, but the transformation that awaits depends on your dedication to utilizing available tools and navigating this icy season.

Loss is not confined to relationships alone; it can also encompass dreams that go unfulfilled. This form of grief, while less overt, carries its own weight. It's as if we're trapped in a cold and barren season, left to grapple with the sadness of unachieved aspirations. However, within this season, lies an opportunity for introspection. Just as nature awakens from its slumber, we, too, can harness the dormant energy of unfulfilled dreams, channeling it into fresh ambitions. Much like spring's transformation of winter's chill into new life, loss can ignite creativity and drive, ushering in new ideas, perspectives, and chances for redemption.

Another subtle, yet very real form of loss is the loss of youth. As we age, we engage in introspection, reflecting on life's journey and comparing it to our youthful aspirations. Regrets and missed opportunities surface, raising concerns about the potential for creating the life we envisioned. Does the saying "Youth is wasted on the young" resonate with you? It's not uncommon to wish for different choices in hindsight. However, let's remember that summer teaches us resilience. "Regrettable" choices and past missteps offer invaluable lessons. Just as the sun's rays nurture life, those summer missteps nurtured your capacity to adapt, learn, and forge new paths with renewed purpose. Reflection is essential, allowing us to place people, events, and experiences in perspective. Yet, just as the car's windshield offers a broader view than the rearview mirror, life's journey lies ahead. Make the most of life's windshield—embrace the journey, detours, and all—to ensure you don't miss the beauty and wisdom it holds.

The final type of loss that warrants our attention is the intricate world of family dynamics, often mirroring the mosaic of autumn colors, each family bearing its unique design. Within this intricate pattern, there exist shared threads that transcend ethnic, cultural, and socioeconomic boundaries—threads of dysfunctional, chaotic, and sometimes distant familial relationships. The pain stemming from family bonds unraveling can evoke feelings of profound loss, akin to leaves falling from the family tree. Yet, pain can also emerge from the connections we longed for but never formed. This dichotomy means we might grieve not only what was lost but also what was never discovered.

My own experiences have granted me insight into the complexities of family dynamics, where the transmission of trauma can persist rather than transform, impacting multiple generations. I've also tasted the bitterness of grieving connections that were never nurtured. It's these personal experiences that compel me to address this facet of loss in our journey, with the hope that my story might offer solace and healing to others.

Navigating the transference of generational trauma necessitated unlearning the narratives I had been taught about myself, others, and the world at large. The process demanded seeing myself through my own eyes rather than through the filtered lens of others' perceptions. It entailed observing the world and its people, allowing me to construct my own belief system. To see myself clearly, I had to invest time in getting to know who I truly am, embracing my authentic self.

As I grew and learned, the desire to break the cycle of transgenerational trauma motivated me. While perfection eluded me, I approached parenting and family-building with intentionality. I delved into my own upbringing, not with judgment, but with a quest for understanding. This understanding was crucial—it unearthed motives behind actions and choices.

Addressing my own family's dysfunction, I grappled with the loss of relationships that crumbled, and mourned those I realized I may never have. The pain ran deep, and I carried it as a burden for years. But in time, I realized that this weight needn't define me. This brings to mind the metaphor of the rearview mirror in the car of life. Glancing back is not an exercise in lament; it's a reminder of my journey's distance covered. Today, I revel in my present, attuned to the path ahead, embracing the chapters of my life—the arrivals, departures, and the constants. This perspective is a result of cultivating gratitude, the tool that transforms loss into gains.

All the above narratives converge to illustrate how different forms of loss are woven into an intricate tapestry, much like the interwoven seasons of nature. Each type of loss imparts its distinct shades to our lives, shaping us in diverse yet interconnected ways. Nature endures its cycles of transformation, and so do we. We adapt, evolve, and navigate through the labyrinth of loss, ever resilient in our quest for meaning and healing.

The human experience is marked by an array of losses—big and small, profound and subtle, too many to list in my short letter to you. Still, it is important to remember how these experiences mold us, shaping us into individuals who've weathered the diverse storms of life. By recognizing the common threads that run through these seasons of loss, we equip ourselves with tools to navigate change, to heal, and to evolve. Through the seasons of divorce, unrealized dreams, loss of time or youth, and family discord, we discover the resilience of the human spirit—the capacity to endure, adapt, and emerge stronger on the other side, which is what I want for you.

Afterword

I hope you find the metaphor of the seasons aptly captures the complex journey of grief. Just like the ebb and flow of nature, grief takes us through various emotional landscapes, each with its own challenges and revelations. The "summer of grief" represents a turning point, where acceptance and healing begin to blossom. It is a season of rediscovery, where we find ourselves gradually reconnecting with life and embracing the memories of our departed loved ones with a sense of peace and gratitude.

However, grief does not always operate as our natural seasons, like clockwork, and the complexity of emotions can sometimes overwhelm us. Yet, through acceptance and self-compassion, we can navigate the stormy winters and emerge stronger. The scars of loss may linger, but they serve as a testament to the love shared and the enduring bond with those we have lost. Some say they are reminders of the battles we have survived.

The journey through grief is not without its challenges, especially when facing the aftermath of suicide or some other circumstance that impedes healing. Still, by simplifying complexities and focusing on the present, we can find hope and purpose in transforming our pain into a source of strength for ourselves and others.

Ultimately, the experience of grief is unique to each individual, and there is no "right" way to grieve. But by honoring our emotions, learning from the lessons grief brings, and seeking support from others, we can find peace, joy, and a meaningful life even amidst the seasons of grief. Life moves on, and just like the changing seasons, we too can embrace the beauty of renewal, growth, and resilience as we journey through grief towards the promise of a brighter tomorrow.

Death and loss may announce itself before arriving or take us completely by surprise, but the only way to get through the pain that follows is to move through it. Yet, amidst the seasons of grief, life reveals lessons about ourselves and offers opportunities for growth. Even the most unimaginable experiences can foster growth. So, take time for yourself, stay present, build a support system, and keep moving forward towards your rainbow—a beautiful, fulfilling life that awaits you.

About the Author

S. Andrea Greene is a compassionate and experienced support coach, holding a Bachelor of Arts in Philosophy and a Master of Science in Counseling Psychology. With a profound understanding of the human grief experience, S. Andrea embarked on a journey to support those navigating the challenging path of pain and loss.

As the founder and owner of Soul Survivors Support Services, LLC, S. Andrea has dedicated her career to providing a nurturing environment for individuals and groups seeking peer support after the loss of a loved one. Her organization serves as a beacon of hope for widows, widowers, and others in need of assistance in managing grief and finding a path to healing.

Combining her academic background in philosophy with the deep insights gained from graduate studies in counseling psychology, S. Andrea has developed a unique and holistic approach to grief support. Her mission is to help individuals embrace the ever-changing seasons of grief, fostering resilience, and facilitating transformative healing.

With a heart-centered approach, S. Andrea has touched the lives of many, offering solace and empowerment to those who have experienced loss. Her commitment to supporting others on their grief journey extends beyond the pages of this book, making her a trusted and compassionate guide in times of heartache.

Through *The Four Seasons of Grief,* S. Andrea shares her wisdom, knowledge, and empathetic guidance, inviting readers to embark on a transformative journey towards healing, hope, and renewal.

Made in the USA
Columbia, SC
16 September 2023

22902390R10059